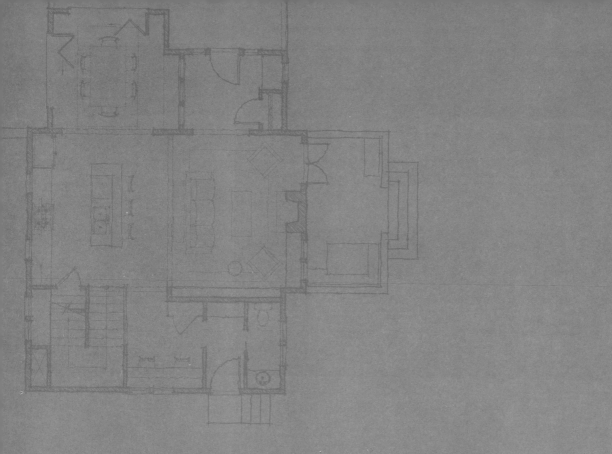
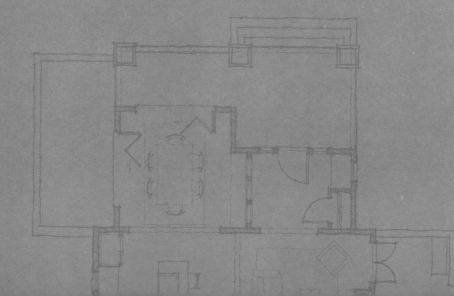

SMALL BUNGALOWS

SMALL BUNGALOWS

CHRISTIAN GLADU

PHOTOGRAPHY BY ROSS CHANDLER

Gibbs Smith, Publisher
TO ENRICH AND INSPIRE HUMANKIND
Salt Lake City | Charleston | Santa Fe | Santa Barbara

To all of the artisan builders who have made bungalows a timeless and integral part of America's Urban Fabric.

First Edition
11 10 09 08 07   5 4 3 2 1

Published by
Gibbs Smith, Publisher
P.O. Box 667
Layton, Utah 84041

Orders: 1.800.835.4993
www.gibbs-smith.com

Designed by Dawn DeVries Sokol
Printed and bound in China

Library of Congress Cataloging-in-Publication Data
Gladu, Christian.
  Small bungalows
Christian Gladu ; Photographs by Ross Chandler. — 1st ed.
    p. cm.
  ISBN-13: 978-1-4236-0098-5
  ISBN-10: 1-4236-0098-3
  1. Bungalows—United States—Designs and plans. 2. Small houses—United States—Designs and plans. 3. Arts and crafts movement—United States—Influence. I. Title.

NA7571.G595 2007
728'.373—dc22
                    2007011258

CONTENTS

ACKNOWLEDGMENTS

A sincere thank-you to Joey Terry for managing and collaborating on the creative content of this book—I value your insight and commitment to this project.

Thank you to the staff at The Bungalow Company for supporting the effort required to produce this book. The projects illustrated in this book would not be possible without your daily commitment to your craft.

To Ross and Pam Chandler—thank you for your professionalism and dedication on this project; your photographs complete the story and have taught me a new way to view the work.

To Rob Leanna—thank you for bringing my ideas to life with your elegant and timeless watercolor renderings. The paintings you created are exactly what we intended for the illustrations section of this book.

I want to thank the home owners who opened their doors and allowed us to share their homes for this project:

Don Ball
Ken and Val Brodeck
Leanne and Chris Champion
Casey Crisler
Peter Guida
Christi Haynes
Beth and Geoff Hobart
Jennifer Helm

Shari and Andy Miller
Brian Maury
Paulette and Rod Page
Kathy Steinert and Paul Haigh
Brian Wasserman
Judy and Jeff Welch
Patsy and Bernie Wolfe

Thank you to the builders and craftsmen whose hard work and dedication to their craft maintain and enhance the spirit of the bungalow.

Thank you to my family for all of your support and patience throughout this process.

INTRODUCTION

The year is 2006, over one hundred years from the inception of the early American Arts and Crafts bungalow. Two world wars, two cars per household, the invention of radio, television, computers and space travel, and we are still talking about the bungalow. There have been many advances in technology; however, the bungalow is etched in American culture with its sensible proportioning and sense of history. The bungalow currently exceeds its initial popularity by years and is treasured in neighborhoods throughout America.

While one of the largest building booms in this country's history occurs, developers strive to create an inventory of new homes and neighborhoods that embody the character, detail and sense of place that keep historic bungalows in demand. The question has to be asked, why the bungalow? The bungalow is a true reflection of our culture, and like any art form, trend or technology, it has been forced to morph to accurately reflect our time.

Architecture is the barometer of culture, artistically reflecting the social and economic fitness of our times. America is returning to urban planning principles that were the foundation of the American bungalow movement. Higher land density coupled with neighborhoods that are located in areas close to public transportation, jobs and community services are large steps in creating communities and neighborhoods that build connections to place and reduce the dependency on the automobile. In creating new communities that draw from history, how do we graciously incorporate today's modern housing requirements and expectations into an urban model that is reflective of planning principles that are over one hundred years old?

At the point original bungalow communities were at their height in America, the automobile was in its infancy. Vehicles were small, and it would have been unlikely for families to have more than one of them. Today, the majority of homes have a two-car garage with room for storage and utilities. Ironically, many garages rival or exceed original bungalows in massing and scale. Additionally, basic homes have grown substantially in size from the turn of the century. Families have decreased in size, but the house has increased in square footage and overall cubic mass. The challenge becomes how, as a culture, do we balance our wants and needs while creating thoughtful design solutions reflective of our time.

THE LAND

CREATING BUILDINGS IN HARMONY WITH NATURE AND PLACE begins with taking time to understand your site. In the fast-paced world of building, it is easy to overlook what attributes the site has and to view them as obstacles. Take the time to truly understand the site, to embrace the features as opportunities, and to learn from the land what the house can be. As you view the home as an enhancement to the land by valuing the surroundings, and as you consciously work with the natural features, you are on the path to integrating the home into the site, not manipulating the site to the house.

Property Survey

Any building site should have a survey drawing identifying the property corners, adjacent roads, easements, environmentally sensitive areas, critical slope and a legal description of the property. This survey will be prepared and stamped by a licensed surveyor verifying that the property corners are accurate and all easements have been recorded.

Site Utilities

The surveyor should locate all site utilities: public sewer, public water, telephone, power and cable television. In the event the site is rural or unimproved, locate adjacent wells, on-site septic systems and site drainage systems. On-site sewer and water systems are normally regulated by county or state. Prior to investing in the land, make sure you clearly understand the requirements for on-site sewer, water and drainage systems; it will directly impact if, and where, you can build on your site.

Topography & Site Features

In addition to the standard survey, a topographical survey of the property is recommended. Topography identifies the slope and terrain of the property depicted in one-foot increments. Slope on a site is easy to misinterpret with the naked eye and is crucial to the integration of house to site. Understanding the topography will also facilitate a straightforward understanding of how to access the site and properly drain it. If your site is treed or has natural features, such as rock outcroppings, it is advisable to have the surveyor locate trees on the map by species and size, and illustrate the locations of the natural features.

ZONING

Every jurisdiction has rules and regulations related to how a building is set on the site and how the building is massed. These rules vary from community to community and are important in determining the design of your home. Schedule an appointment with your city or county planner and have them explain the regulations. As you start the design process, bring back your schematic concepts and review your understanding of the regulations and how you have applied them to your design. Working with the planner right from the start will reduce the likelihood of having to rework your design; it is much easier to adjust the design during the schematic phase than once you have completed the design and documentation process. Zoning is definitely not a simple or logical path, but you can save yourself time, money and frustration by understanding the rules before you buy property and begin your design and construction process.

DESIGN COVENANTS, CONDITIONS & RESTRICTIONS

In addition to zoning, many neighborhoods have a set of design regulations that overlay the zoning code; many times you are required to adhere to both sets of rules. Neighborhood rules relate

EVERY JURISDICTION HAS RULES AND REGULATIONS RELATED TO HOW A BUILDING IS SET ON THE SITE AND HOW THE BUILDING IS MASSED.

to style, allowable materials, minimum and maximum allowable square footages, landscaping plans and operational rules of living in the neighborhood. These rules are a legal contract and require compliance with the designated design review board. It is customary for the developer to take a deposit that ensures compliance with the approved plans.

Site Planning

It is a good idea to create a drawing showing all elements of the site before beginning the design process. Making visual notes on the drawing to identify the path of the sun, the direction of prevailing weather, the views, and key elements of the site that you want to enhance or maintain, aide in creating a logical design for the site. Prior to beginning the actual design of the home, lay out options for pedestrian and vehicular access to the site. Good documentation of the site and thorough understanding of the site's features will not only make the home more attractive and functional, but can save thousands in construction dollars.

It is a good idea to create a drawing showing all elements of the site before beginning the design process.

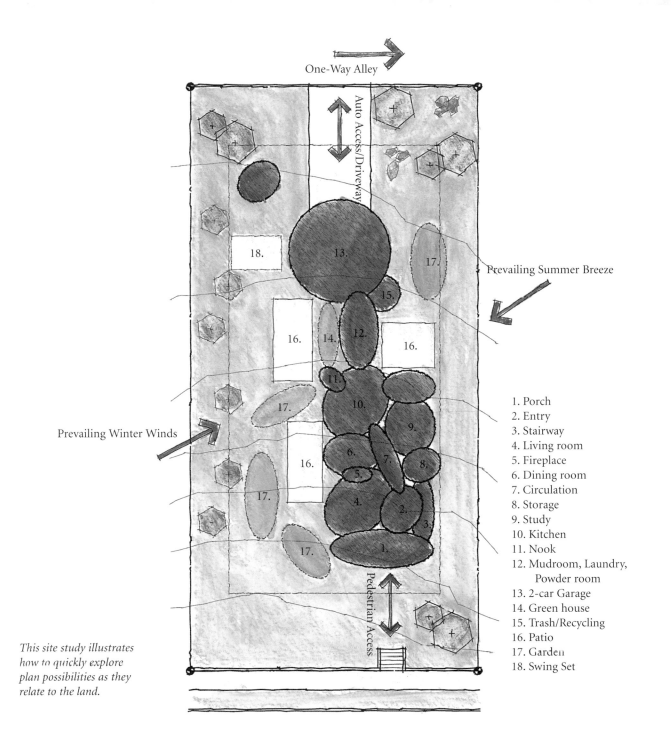

One-Way Alley

Auto Access/Driveway

Prevailing Summer Breeze

Prevailing Winter Winds

Pedestrian Access

1. Porch
2. Entry
3. Stairway
4. Living room
5. Fireplace
6. Dining room
7. Circulation
8. Storage
9. Study
10. Kitchen
11. Nook
12. Mudroom, Laundry,
    Powder room
13. 2-car Garage
14. Green house
15. Trash/Recycling
16. Patio
17. Garden
18. Swing Set

*This site study illustrates
how to quickly explore
plan possibilities as they
relate to the land.*

The bungalow porch, whether rural or urban, is the transitional space from the exterior to the interior.

BUNGALOW INTERIOR

THE BUNGALOW INTERIOR IS A COLLECTION of interdependent spaces woven together with handcrafted details, establishing an intimate sense of scale to the home. The front porch is the transition from the outside elements to the built environment, where its materials and details set the stage for what can be expected on the interior of the home. Marking the entry to the home, the porch provides a space for welcoming visitors. The porch serves as a greeting portal to the home and doubles as an exterior living space that reaches out to the community, working as a casual gathering place for friends and neighbors. It is the exterior space that envelops the outdoors and invites the landscape into the home.

An entry with sidelights allows the inhabitants to connect visually with visitors.

THE ENTRY

Entering a bungalow begins at the front porch and transitions into an entry space that creates a barrier from the elements and a space to decompress before entering the living space. The entry also functions as a place to store seasonal coats and shoes, and has evolved as a place to leave behind reminders of the hectic day, like cell phones and car keys, before escaping into the home. An entry to a porch with high windows in the door or sidelights helps inhabitants connect visually with visitors or strangers prior to opening the door. Even in the smallest of homes, an obvious entry helps organize the coming and going of a family's daily routine and provides a sense of privacy to interior spaces.

The front porch provides a clear point of entry while the side porch allows for outdoor space for family entertainment.

The entry also functions as a place to store seasonal coats and shoes.

THE LIVING ROOM

The living room is located adjacent to the entry and has a visual and physical connection to the porch. The flow of these areas is about building a hierarchy of space and locating more of the open space to public sides of the home. Bungalows were commonly located on deep and narrow lots, which made the orientation of living rooms, dens and dining rooms towards the street side of the home, and focused on pushing bedrooms and bathrooms upstairs or to the rear of the lot. Ironically, the bungalow fireplace may be rivaled only by the front porch in terms of what makes us "think bungalow." The fireplace was typically centered on an outside wall flanked by high windows and bookcases. Even with the invention of television, stereo and computers, the fireplace has been able to stand its ground as the focal point of the living room.

Flanking bookcases have evolved into areas to incorporate televisions and stereo equipment that can be integrated gracefully behind folding doors. In bungalows there is still a strong inclination to maintain the

Site-crafted tile combined with fir millwork creates a warm and intimate living room.

THE BUNGALOW FIREPLACE MAY BE RIVALED ONLY BY THE FRONT PORCH IN TERMS OF WHAT MAKES US "THINK BUNGALOW."

French doors from the adja-cent den allow for back-lighting the living room.

living room as sanctuary for conversing, reading and socializing, so media equipment is alternatively located in dens or other play areas. Small bungalows strongly rely on the integration of light and a connection to the exterior of the home to create smaller spaces that live large. Living rooms and other public spaces rely on getting direct light from at least two outside window direc-tions while creating views to the outside landscape. Additionally, a visual connection to other public spaces like kitchens and din-ing rooms provides more back lighting and a link to the outdoors.

The transition between public spaces is delineated with a change in ceiling height or a cased opening detailed with millwork that relates to window and door trim. Cased openings and varied ceiling heights work in conjunction with the ceiling treatment as part of the road map that identifies and reinforces the use of the space. Cased openings provide opportunities for a change in color or

Visual connection from the living room to the dining room creates a continuous flow between spaces.

finish material, which initiates a transition through the public spaces. Treatments, such as boxed beams, built-in bookcases and columns, give the room organization and provide a logical pathway for lighting fixtures and furniture arrangement.

Transition between public and private space is delineated with a change in ceiling height or a cased opening detailed with millwork that relates to window and door trim.

FAR RIGHT: *Flanked columns and a change in floor heights create a distinct definition between spaces.*

FAR LEFT AND ABOVE: *Use of indigenous Carderock stone links bungalow interior to its natural landscape.*

LEFT: *Here is an example of Greene and Greene–inspired joinery on a fireplace mantel.*

THE DINING ROOM

One hundred years ago, the dining room was the breaking point from public to private spaces and commonly bordered the kitchen with a solid wall, built-in, pass-through or sideboard. Occasionally, the dining room had integrated storage for china and linens and a bank of three to four windows. Depending on the orientation of the home to the adjacent neighbor, these windows may have been high and located over the sideboard. Wainscot or chair rail often clad the room, providing a sense of identity to the dining room. The top of the wainscot would

Historically inspired textiles soften the room both visually and acoustically.

Wainscot or chair rail often clads the dining room, providing a sense of identity.

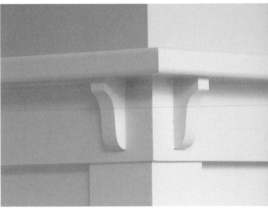

The top of the wainscot sometimes incorporates a plate rail that functions as a place to display pottery or other decorative arts.

incorporate a plate rail that functioned as a place to display pottery or other decorative arts. As the center for family meals, the dining room has been redefined in the bungalow renaissance as a subspace of the kitchen, and has been included as a function within, or adjacent to, the kitchen. An attribute of the dining room is the integration of additional natural light, as the shared wall between the kitchen and dining room has been removed, unveiling a continual visual connection through the entire main floor. As outdoor entertainment and cooking have become a more prototypical activity in American culture, the connection to the outdoors has also become a more integrated pattern in the function of the dining room.

As the center for family meals, the dining room has been redefined in the bungalow renaissance as a subspace of the kitchen.

FAR LEFT: *The kitchen, once an isolated workroom for the strict purpose of storing, cooking and preparing food, has morphed into the heart of the home.*

An attribute of the dining room is the integration of additional natural light as the shared wall between the kitchen and dining room has been removed, unveiling a continual visual connection through the entire main floor.

THE KITCHEN

The kitchen, once an isolated workroom for the strict purpose of storing, cooking and preparing food, has morphed into the heart of the home. Hierarchy of all public space is planned around the connection to the kitchen. Even in a simple remodel, connecting the kitchen to the other public spaces can revolutionize a once bland diagram. Food preparation has evolved since the 1920s and families now spend less time preparing basic food and more time refining their culinary techniques.

The kitchen revolution has taken the kitchen full circle, from an isolated utilitarian work area to a fully integrated public space.

THE KITCHEN REVOLUTION

Bridging the gap between urban and agrarian life in the 1920s, the bungalow kitchen was a derivative of a farm kitchen. A kitchen was lucky to have running water, electricity or refrigeration. Root cellars were still common, and even bungalows on small urban lots integrated kitchen gardens into the landscape. The kitchen revolution has taken the kitchen full circle, from an isolated utilitarian work area to a fully integrated public space. Arts and Crafts–inspired millwork and joinery celebrate the spirit of the craft. Integrating modern appliances into Stickley-esque cabinetry, and cladding the work surfaces with indigenous stone material, philosophically unites modern kitchens with their past.

LEFT: *Integrated nook and coffee station reduces crossed traffic patterns.*

ABOVE: *The Glasow Rose inlay of rosewood and American cherry pay homage to design elements of the early American Arts and Crafts movement.*

ABOVE RIGHT: *Traditional Arts and Crafts joinery and hardware celebrate a furniture-like approach to kitchen design.*

RIGHT: *Decorative cherry brackets support cabinets.*

ABOVE: *Slate with integrated tile creates a pattern that unites nature with handmade crafts.*

RIGHT: *Cladding the work surfaces with indigenous stone material philosophically unites modern kitchens with their past.*

FAR RIGHT: *This shows integration of modern appliances into Stickley-esque cabinetry.*

A kitchen island serves as a gathering place for guest and cook, promoting cooking as a social activity.

Open shelves allow for display of pottery and dishes.

Tile backsplashes, countertops and floors are now palettes to reinvent. They pay homage to the highly crafted tile and pottery guilds so crucial to the Arts and Crafts movement.

THE NOOK

Historically, the nook was located in the kitchen and was fairly utilitarian. It was simply a place to have a quick breakfast or lunch and was not adequately sized for a big meal. As the kitchen has become part of the central core of the home and as lifestyles have become more hectic, the nook now functions as a family dining area. Additionally, the nook serves as a public space to do homework, have a cup of coffee with a friend or plan the weekly meals. Nooks incorporate seating from four to six people and are now constructed of furniture-quality materials with integrated storage under the seat. Nooks can be located on interior or exterior walls and create an opportunity to use additional windows in the kitchen without adversely affecting upper cabinet storage. In some smaller bungalow plans, the nook has fully replaced the traditional dining room and has been incorporated with a nautical quality.

Nooks built with furniture-quality materials and craftsmanship pay tribute to original bungalow built-ins.

RIGHT: *In smaller bungalow plans, the nook has fully replaced the traditional dining room and has been incorporated with a nautical quality.*

Built-in nook bench, in collaboration with a small dining room table, blends the nook with the dining room.

THE BUTLER'S PANTRY

The butler's pantry has evolved into the chef's desk and is a small, semiprivate space out of sight to pay bills, catch up on e-mail and keep homework in order. The butler's pantry functions as a boundary where work and the link to the outside world can be organized and put away when necessary.

Pantries work as auxiliary spaces to the kitchen and are highly successful in storing bulk food, seldom-used portable appliances and even less attractive appliances such as microwaves and coffeemakers. The walk-in pantry is flexible, durable and less expensive to build than furniture-inspired cabinetry. A well-located and orderly pantry can store all food and let the kitchen cabinets function as a toolbox to arrange utensils and cookware. Designing the kitchen around straightforward traffic patterns—like storing all food in the pantry, all pots and pans in pull-out cabinet drawers and dishes in locations out of the cooking traffic pattern—lets the smallest kitchen function smoothly and efficiently. Clear traffic patterns allow everyone to participate in the preparation and clean up of meals. Planning a kitchen diagram that allows for kitchen cleanup based on working from dirty to clean and directly to the storage cabinet, can reduce clean-up time and crossed traffic patterns.

Cabinetry can be custom designed around appliances such as coffeemakers and drink or wine

The butler's pantry functions as a boundary where work and the link to the outside world can be organized and put away when necessary.

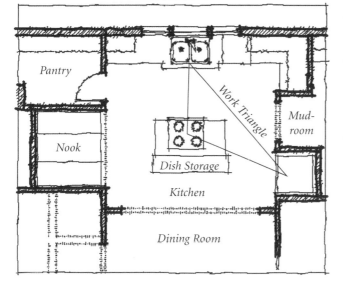

ABOVE LEFT: *The nook provides the ability to eat in the kitchen without conflicting with work patterns.*

ABOVE RIGHT: *Dishes are located out of the cooking traffic pattern, which lets the smallest kitchen function smoothly and efficiently.*

LEFT: *Kitchen diagram illustrates efficient traffic patterns and work flow.*

Pantry

Nook

Work Triangle

Mud-
room

Dish Storage

Kitchen

Dining Room

RIGHT: *Cabinetry can be custom designed around appliances such as coffee-makers and drink or wine refrigerators.*

BELOW: *Locating the kitchen adjacent to an exterior entrance and to an outdoor room establishes a seasonal and climatic flow to the outside cooking and entertaining areas.*

refrigerators. Locating functions not essential to meal preparation out of main traffic patterns will ease the flow of a small work space and maintain adequate refrigerator and freezer space for food. The kitchen instinctively works as the heart of the home, creating distinct traffic patterns for both cook and guests. Locating the kitchen adjacent to an exterior entrance and to an outdoor room establishes a seasonal and climatic flow to outside cooking and entertaining areas.

Found objects, like this antique cabinet, bring a stylized and personal touch to the powder room of a traditional bungalow.

The mudroom serves as an exit to the backyard, as an entrance to an attached or detached garage, and as a storage facility for shoes and coats.

THE MUDROOM

The mudroom has become a necessity in more extreme climates. Original bungalows were located in neighborhoods that were designed with narrow and deep lots where vehicular access was from an alley. Today, circulation patterns from the rear of the house require an additional decompression zone for stowing backpacks, coats and mail. The mudroom serves as an exit to the

Use of obscured glass in a powder room introduces natural light while maintaining privacy.

backyard, as an entrance to an attached or detached garage and as a storage facility for shoes and coats. The mudroom also functions as a laundry center and as a logical space to put garments used for gardening, exercise or outdoor play. With the direct attachment to the kitchen, the mudroom allows efficiency for busy families as they prepare a meal in the kitchen while working in a load of laundry. A mudroom cabinet can be used as an area to charge cell phones and organize mail—a key element to providing a layer of sanity between family and the outside world. The mail center should also incorporate adequate areas for recycling trash generated from sorting the mail. Introducing a downstairs bath or powder room accessed off or adjacent to the mudroom allows for a private and tucked-away solution for family and guests. It also discourages children or would-be gardeners from navigating the entire house in search of a bathroom.

The Den

Usually, the den was set up for reading and private away time. Dens in newer homes are set up for library storage and a larger work-at-home space. In many new bungalows, dens function as play areas for small children, or places to work on art projects. Many families have chosen to control and limit exposure to various media, essentially relocating the television from the primary living areas to a separate media area for viewing television and movies. The den functions well for this use due to its smaller size, which provides the ability to control light and sound. The invention of flat-screen monitors and smaller audio

Dens in newer homes are set up for library storage and a larger work-at-home space.

LEFT: *Small work spaces within the den can function as great home offices.*

RIGHT: While many bungalow families choose to combine work space with the den, this office is located adjacent to the den.

This area functions as an at-home work studio, a play space and as toy storage.

visual components has reduced the space requirements for media, which lets even a well-appointed media room still function as a play area or home office. Designating a specific area for entertainment helps control the overall acoustics and intrusion that can be introduced into the home through unmonitored media.

THE STAIRCASE

The staircase is many times an afterthought in the design of a new bungalow but is a key element in the design of any small home. The staircase is ultimately a vertical room connecting the public spaces of a home to the more intimate family spaces such as bedrooms and bathrooms. Staircases in small homes need to be generous in width and have a comfortable run-to-rise ratio to facilitate uninhibited flow up and down. Typically, bungalows with second floors have stairs located at the entry and, in most cases, on an exterior wall. Narrow lot design of the bungalow does not usually allow for the centrally located staircases of colonial, cape or farmhouses. Plan-book bungalows vary in width from twenty-four to thirty feet. If a four-foot staircase is centered, it would leave rooms from ten to twelve feet on each side. Generally, public spaces need to be fourteen to sixteen feet wide. Centering the staircase also creates a dark wall in the center of the home, which breaks the visual connection to the outdoors and confines the space. A staircase situated on an outside wall allows the primary

Typically, bungalows with second floors have stairs located at the entry and, in most cases, on an exterior wall.

A STAIRCASE SITUATED ON AN OUTSIDE WALL ALLOWS THE PRIMARY PUBLIC SPACES TO RECEIVE NATURAL BACKLIGHT AND A CONNECTION TO OUTDOORS WHILE MAINTAINING PRIVACY.

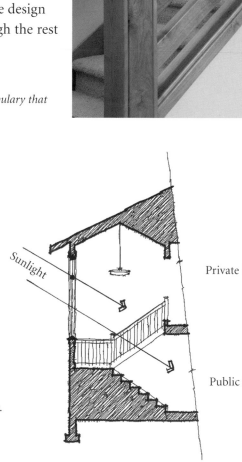

public spaces to receive natural backlight and a connection to outdoors while maintaining privacy. It is one of the most interesting rooms in any home. It is an ideal place to display books, family photos and collectibles. It establishes the design vocabulary that is carried through the rest of the home.

The staircase establishes the design vocabulary that is carried through the rest of the home.

ABOVE: *Windows at the stair landing provide natural light to the entry and other public spaces.*

Stair newel marks transition from public to private spaces.

RIGHT: *A staircase situated on an outside wall allows the primary public spaces to receive natural backlight and a connection to outdoors while maintaining privacy.*

Sunlight

Private Spaces

Public Spaces

Bedrooms

Bungalow bedrooms are a reflection of the overall scale of the home. If a bedroom is for a child or teenager, it needs to be a minimum of ten by ten feet. If one dimension is a little smaller, the other dimension can be a little longer. The dimensions can be much smaller if the room is used as an infant's nursery that will be converted later into a craft room, reading room or home office.

Bedroom closets can be integrated into the room either with sliding or bi-fold doors or with a single door to a walk-in closet. The use of a full-swing door is cumbersome in small spaces and limits furniture placement and flow throughout the room. The integrated room closet needs to have a pair of doors between four and five feet wide, maximum. The organization of the interior of the closet is a key element to a smaller bedroom. Contracting a closet specialist is a great way to maximize storage and have age-appropriate design solutions for clothing storage. The cost of having a closet outfitter is fairly inexpensive and the hardware is flexible, so as the storage needs of the child evolve, so can the closet system. If space allows, a walk-in

The integrated room closet needs to have a pair of doors between four and five feet wide, maximum.

closet works well; however, if a walk-in closet is not at least four by five feet inside, it will actually have less storage than the traditional integrated closet. The benefit of a walk-in closet is that it reduces the number of doors in the room—this ultimately lightens up the flow pattern in the bedroom.

Bedrooms should also integrate light from at least two directions; the placement of high windows over a bed can be a good way to achieve this. The bedrooms need to be exactly that, a retreat focused on downtime, relaxation and calmness. Creating a space outside of the bedroom for computers and homework lets parents properly supervise computer usage, and it relinquishes the bedroom from office tasks.

Bedrooms should integrate light from at least two directions; the placement of high windows over a bed can be a good way to achieve this.

dream

gro[

Creating a space outside of the bedroom for computers and homework lets parents properly supervise computer usage, and it relinquishes the bedroom from office tasks.

JACK AND JILL
BATHROOMS, ACCESSED
ONLY FROM EACH
BEDROOM, CAN REDUCE
A HALLWAY DOOR AND
MAKE EACH BEDROOM
FUNCTION AS A
SMALL SUITE.

The modern master bedroom occasionally includes built-in fireplaces, roof decks or reading areas.

BATHROOMS

If a bathroom is shared by two or more bedrooms, compartmentalizing the bathroom allows more than one person to use the bathroom at a time, expediting the flow of the daily routine. Separating the tub and water closet from the sink area gives full privacy to the bath and partial privacy for sink activities. Designing a bathroom cabinet with adequate storage for towels and bathroom supplies helps clear the vanity for daily use. Jack and Jill bathrooms, accessed only from each bedroom, can reduce a hallway door and make each bedroom function as a small suite. The negative to this is the need to plan for an additional door, which, if not well laid out, can create a gridlock of doors. Many designs solve the additional door issue with the use of pocket doors; however, pocket doors are not good at isolating sound and could be disturbing to the adjacent bedroom. For safety reasons, parents should consider if young children should have an unsupervised entrance to a bathroom.

THE MASTER BEDROOM

The master bedroom was foreign to original bungalows but has become a major focus in new American housing. The master bedroom requires a private entrance to the bathroom and to a walk-in closet or multiple in-wall closets. Storage needs have grown as both husband and wife have entered the work

force and families spend their free time enjoying outdoor activities. Sporting activities require specific clothing and accessories, which increase storage requirements. The master bedroom has become more than just a place for sleeping. The modern master bedroom occasionally includes built-in fireplaces, roof decks or reading areas.

The master bedroom should have room for a king- or queen-sized bed, nightstands, a dresser and a small conversation area. Creating flexible storage in the master bedroom lets a bookshelf cross over to sweater or linen storage with the use of decorative containers; a wall of storage helps store collectibles, family photos and books. An integrated window seat, much like an original inglenook, provides an area to sit and read in privacy while capturing second-story views.

Creating flexible storage in the master bedroom lets a bookshelf cross over to sweater or linen storage with the use of decorative containers.

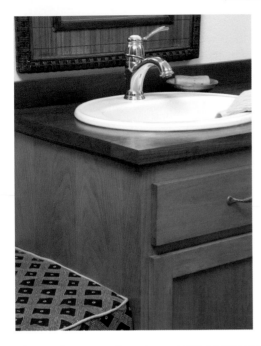

THE MASTER BATHROOM

The master bath is accessed privately from the master bedroom. The traditional claw-foot tub has been replaced with a walk-in tiled shower and compartmentalized water closet. Many times the vanity includes double sinks with cabinetry below to store supplies and towels. The master bath relies on high, private windows to create a well-lit and ventilated bathroom. In larger master bathrooms, a soaking tub is used in addition to a walk-in shower, providing a private space to unwind. Master closets are typically accessed through the master bath, reducing the disturbance created when couples keep different schedules.

The use of a variety of woods creates a feeling of warmth.

RIGHT: *In larger master bathrooms, a soaking tub is used in addition to a walk-in shower, providing a private space to unwind.*

GREENING THE BUNGALOW

Standing the Test of Time

Smaller residences require fewer resources to build, less energy to run, and work in harmony with the land; this ultimately creates a flexible housing stock that will grow with our culture and be a solid framework for future generations. Even the most well-intentioned or best-constructed home, with the most efficient systems and best solar orientation, still needs to work within the context of its surroundings in order to be a permanent thread of the urban fabric.

Home construction, in general, is not a green practice by nature, and it takes vast amounts of resources and energy to produce the most basic structure. Of course, if natural resources are going to be used, it is imperative that we make the best use of natural resources. It has been proven that with sound construction methods and appropriate climatic detailing, the buildings are guaranteed to stand the test of time as well as the forces of nature. Buildings as fluid structures will evolve over generations when properly maintained, and by utilizing simple, indigenous and natural materials, they will remain healthy as they respond to the local environment. If well proportioned and sympathetically integrated in the land, the home will be readapted, not demolished or rebuilt in less than thirty years.

Integrity in Building Conservatively

Conservation is the most straightforward approach to reducing energy consumption, easily applied to every new home built today, without having to retool or invest in complicated equipment. Smaller, well-insulated homes readily achieve this with proper orientation that harnesses the sun's energy. Innovative principles in building become more achievable when land developers, city jurisdictions and designers work together to plan communities where jobs are attainable to support the houses being produced, thus reducing single-occupant car trips and, ultimately, dependency on fossil fuels. To bridge the environmental gap, fossil fuel should be the alternative energy source, not the primary source.

A Conservative Approach to Neighborhood Planning

New urbanism is a powerful tool in planning new communities that are pedestrian friendly and less reliant on car trips and fossil fuel consumption. By creating density to reduce urban sprawl, acute planners will plan communities that work with the solar orientation of the land. As solar energy establishes a foothold in the American energy market, innovative developers will mandate that all homes incorporate active and/or passive solar technology into their designs. By designing new homes to harness the sun's energy and to reduce energy consumption by building smaller and more efficiently, a conservation trend will be set and will ultimately reduce America's dependency on foreign energy.

By encouraging the embrace between building, landscape and gardens, the structure will integrate over time.

BUNGALOW EXTERIOR

THE BUNGALOW IS AN EXTENSION of its natural surroundings. It reflects indigenous wood and stone and, with time, integrates itself with the surrounding landscape. As the landscape matures and the house shows signs of wear, the house and the site appear as one. Initially, new homes feel stark on the site—so by encouraging the embrace between building, landscape and gardens, the structure will eventually integrate into its environment.

Originally, bungalows were built on rock foundations, or coursed with brick above finished grade. The use of more durable indigenous materials at the base of the building creates a natural transition between the land and the built environment. Modern construction methods include building homes on reinforced-concrete foundations that can be veneered with masonry or parged with cemented plaster to build a connection between earth and home.

When the garage is accessed from the front of the home and below grade, it creates an auto court of indigenous rock, which allows for a durable solution for the car-to-house transition. To do this, you can incorporate site stairs from the auto court to the porch of rock and cut stone treads.

RIGHT: *This Bungalow illustrates the marriage between nature and home.*

SIDING

Bungalow siding is often composed of clapboards and cedar shingles; however, in some specific regions, brick or stucco is common. The bungalow is truly an architectural chameleon, adapting its universal architectural form to work with regional building techniques, traditions, environmental conditions and personal expressions. Bungalows are generally one story to one-and-a-half stories and are likely to change materials at the water table, the eaves line and the transition between floors.

In situations where the bungalow stands four to six steps off the natural grade, shingle or lap siding would be used. This transition of materials is normally separated with a water table—a milled piece of wood designed to shed the water from the wall plane above and create a horizontal band on the building, which then reinforces the horizontal massing of the building.

Material change between floors is accomplished by building up multiple courses of shingles that generate a shadow line. This gives the shingles the appearance of floating while visually lightening the second story. Building up the bottom course of shingles forces water to the outside of the building and sheds it to the ground, reducing the tendency of the water to migrate behind the wall and damage the structure. Alternatively, a belt band or belly band may be used to make the

Belly bands can be used at the base of the building, in lieu of the water table, or at any other horizontal material change on the building.

Use of exposed timbers exemplifies the roots of the bungalow.

A decorative bracket supports barge rafter while the belly band delineates a change in materials.

Bungalows are generally one story to one-and-a-half stories and are likely to change materials at the water table, eaves line and the transition between floors.

horizontal transition between siding materials. Belly bands can be used at the base of the building, in lieu of the water table, or at any other horizontal material change on the building.

Lap siding, or clapboard, is installed with three- to six-inch exposure and either terminates into corner boards at the outside corners or is mitered. Mitered corners are very common in traditional bungalows; however, this detail is highly susceptible to water damage. Newer composite materials are not able to be mitered but provide metal corner transition caps, which are still not water tight.

Unique to bungalow- and prairie-style homes, lap siding and shingles are commonly installed with alternating patterns. An example of this would be two clapboards at three-inch exposure and three clapboards at five-inch exposure, producing a repeat pattern of five.

VENTED GABLES

In hot climates, attic and roof ventilation was originally incorporated into gable ends. Gable-end vents were openings in the structure covered with screens to protect the home from insects. The screened openings were covered with decorative latticework, which provided an additional layer of detail. New bungalows are commonly vented from the roof at the eaves with a vented freeze block and again with a continuously vented ridge. Incorporating latticework in the gables breaks down the overall scale of the building and produces elegant shadows.

Use of the same material in different colors breaks down the scale of the bungalow.

LEFT: *Incorporating latticework in the gables produces elegant shadows.*

ROOFING

Bungalow roofs are made of several integrated roof forms. Multiple roof forms reduce the overall mass of the building while establishing visual interest.

One-and-a-half-story bungalows create rooms under the shelter of the roof, which allows the roof forms to read through to the interior.

A gable roof form defines this master bedroom and adds visual interest.

The roof structure is supported with roof brackets or outriggers that connect to the building walls and support the barge rafters, giving the appearance of the roof hovering over the building.

Multiple roof forms reduce the overall mass of the building.

Bungalow roofs are made of several integrated roof forms.

BELOW LEFT: *Two- to four-foot overhangs are supported with exposed rafter tails and reveal exposed soffit material.*

BELOW CENTER: *The roof structure is supported with roof brackets, or outriggers, that connect to the building walls and support the barge rafters, giving the appearance of the roof hovering over the building.*

Unique patterns used at gable ends create a signature look.

Custom wall treatment mimics rafter tail design and integrates the roof to the walls.

Barge rafter tails, adorned with decorative patterns cut into two by twelve-foot timbers, produce an artistic termination to the roof.

Two- to four-foot overhangs are supported with exposed rafter tails and reveal exposed soffit material, reinforcing the layered effect of the bungalow roof. Barge rafter tails, adorned with decorative patterns cut into two by twelve-foot timbers, produce an artistic termination to the roof.

Roof gutters were originally wood and cut into the rafter tails for support. Five-inch half-round gutters made of formed aluminum or copper are more common in modern construction. Often, round downspouts are replaced with metal chains, which tie to concealed drains. The chains are allowed to patina, reinforcing the bungalow's connection with nature.

Roof gutters were originally wood and were cut into the rafter tails for support. Five-inch half-round gutters made of formed aluminum or copper are more common in modern construction.

LEFT: Round downspouts are replaced with metal chains, which are allowed to patina, reinforcing the bungalow's connection with nature.

WINDOWS

Historically, bungalow windows were primarily double-hung wood windows that slid in wood tracks and used cylindrical window weights hung from hemp sash cords to counterbalance the operation of the window. Windows were proportioned using a cottage-sash configuration. *Cottage sash* simply means that the top sash of the window is approximately one-third of the overall length of the window. The top window sash contains a variety of horizontal and vertical mullion divisions to create a decorative pattern in the top sash. The lower sash is longer and consists of a single pane of glass.

High windows flanking a fireplace or over a dining room buffet might be leaded stained-glass windows. Leaded-glass transom windows were incorporated in the front elevation of the bungalow as a

VINYL WINDOWS ARE CONSIDERED TO BE LOW MAINTENANCE; HOWEVER, THEY ARE SUSCEPTIBLE TO SAGGING IN THE HEAT AND CRACKING IN THE COLD.

Cottage sash *simply means that the top sash of the window is approximately one-third of the overall length of the window.*

design element. Casement windows are less prevalent but are occasionally integrated in kitchens, bathrooms and closets. Modern windows are still constructe d of wood but are often clad with vinyl or aluminum. Vinyl windows are the most inexpensive and are, in general, limited to four colors—primarily white or tan, and occasionally in green or bronze. Vinyl windows are considered to be low maintenance; however, they are susceptible to sagging in the heat and cracking in the cold. Few vinyl windows have an operable top sash—this is counterintuitive when trying to vent hot air from a room or to cross ventilate. Aluminum clad over wood and vinyl clad over wood both make removable sashes and provide a traditional wood window interior, which is a key element in designing a traditional bungalow interior. Aluminum-clad windows come in a variety of colors and are probably the most durable of all production windows.

Windows are one of the most important decisions when building a new home and are key elements in creating a traditionally inspired bungalow. Windows and doors are literally stitched to the exterior with layers of flashing and decorative trim; they are attached from the inside with fine woodwork and interior finishes. Therefore, an investment in high-quality windows is suggested—they will help to conserve energy and to increase the longevity of the home.

ABOVE LEFT: *Casement windows are less prevalent but are occasionally integrated in kitchens, bathrooms and closets.*

ABOVE: *Aluminum clad over wood and vinyl clad over wood both make removable sashes and provide a wood window interior, which is a key element in designing a traditional bungalow.*

PORCH COLUMNS & RAILINGS

Masonry porch column bases root the porch colonnade to the site.

Masonry porch column bases root the porch to the site, while expressed timber, or tapered wood columns, connect to corresponding lintels that modestly support the roof. Porch roofs are commonly constructed of multiple roof forms, but the entry is highlighted with a gabled roof. The front door is generally centered beneath the ridge and is flanked with windows or a sidelight of decorative or leaded glass. Smaller bungalows are organized with a single door and more modest porch. Porch railings consist of both half-walls and siding, or decorative patterns cut into more substantial wood timber. Brick bungalows use brick coursing or rock for a masonry lattice that separates the porch from the street. Railings of either wood or masonry are substantial enough for visitors to sit and converse.

ABOVE: *Exposed timber columns connect shingled column bases to beams above.*

FACING: *Tapered wood columns connect the roof structure to stone column bases.*

LIGHTING

Bungalows are smaller in scale and less reliant on highly technical lighting fixtures. The interior lighting for a bungalow relies on integrating the style of the fixtures with the interior and exterior details. Natural light always plays a large part in the lighting scheme, but when the sun goes down, natural light will need to be replaced with artificial light.

Spaces in a bungalow are smaller and more intimate by nature; general illumination can be handled with ceiling-mounted fixtures that illuminate the overall space. Small recessed can lights used sparingly can augment ceiling-mounted fixtures for general illumination. Recessed ceiling fixtures may be equipped with baffles that focus the light on objects of art or key architectural elements. Programmable dimmers create a flexible and dramatic lighting effect. Light fixtures can be equipped with a variety of lamps, which are available in different intensity and colors that can significantly affect the coloration of paint and fabrics in the interior environment.

Wall sconces can provide additional general illumination but are best used to develop a pathway up a set of stairs or along a hallway. Sconces can reflect light onto the ceiling for general illumination or down a wall to create a more intimate effect. Potentially, the most important element in designing a lighting scheme is the use of task lighting or lamps. Generating pools of light at the source of use is fundamental in creating a cozy and warm ambience. Providing switched outlets helps control lamp usage when entering or exiting a room.

BUILD WHAT YOU WANT

Designing and building a new bungalow is an opportunity to explore how you currently live your life versus how you would like to live your life. Drawing from life experiences and applying them to the design process brings thought, purpose and specificity to a home; when integrated with reverence for the land, this creates a home of great architecture. Be introspective. Decide what you need and want. Don't be a victim of real estate marketing studies that define what the average person wants. The home you have designed will be for you and your family.

Executing a successful project involves developing a cohesive team between owner, designer and builder. Hiring a design professional is more involved than picking one out of the phone book. Choose a designer based on previous work you have seen, recommendations and a personal connection. A designer is a professional guide through the design process, there to ensure a quality design that meets building standards and is within your budget. Equally important is the selection of a qualified builder. The ideal builder will have experience in building homes that you like, have an established relationship with your designer and have a history of financial responsibility and of projects delivered on time. Clear and honest communication between owner, designer and builder is necessary in meeting all parties' expectations.

Simplicity is the heartbeat of the small bungalow and is the key to building a successful project. Having a home designed and built is much more than obtaining a plan and having a contractor show up and start building. Great buildings that stand the test of time ultimately evolve with culture, technology and lifestyle.

SMALL BUNGALOW PLANS—ILLUSTRATED

DESIGNS BY THE BUNGALOW COMPANY

ARCHITECTURAL ILLUSTRATIONS BY ROB LEANNA

THE FOLLOWING EIGHT SMALL BUNGALOWS and two garages are designed to work in traditionally designed neighborhoods, on infill lots in historic neighborhoods and on rural property. The intent of these designs is to create a new small bungalow that reflects the lifestyle of today's families. The designs, inspired by the principles in this book, are focused on reinterpreting the ideals and principles of the bungalow for this century. Creating smaller homes with flexible spaces allows the integration of new technology into bungalows while maintaining a dedication to the detail and craftsmanship that defines the bungalow. It is our hope that these homes will serve as an inspiration for a new generation of home buyer who is truly in search of the not-so-big house.

THE ZINNIA

First floor: 948 square feet
Second floor: 760 square feet
Total: 1,708 square feet

This classically styled three-bedroom bungalow is planned so that outdoor rooms flow from the interior. The Zinnia is designed to work in traditional neighborhood developments as a new home on an infill lot. The open plan integrates all public living space visually, while cased openings and varied ceiling heights create a hierarchy of spaces. An at-home work space is located adjacent to the stair and allows for natural light to filter from above, back-lighting the kitchen area. The second floor houses a master suite, two bedrooms, a central hall bath and a laundry center. The master bedroom includes a walk-in closet and full bath with walk-in shower. The master bedroom connects to a second-story deck, providing a private connection to the outdoors.

The Zinnia

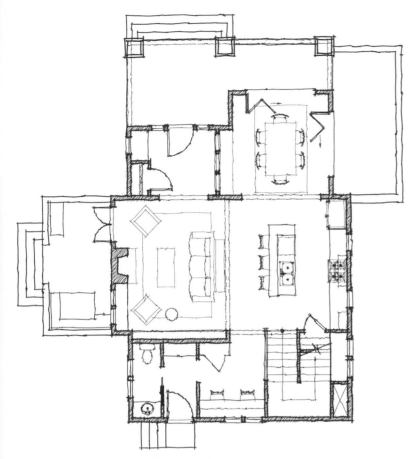

The Zinnia First Floor

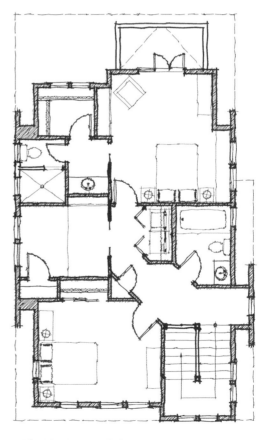

The Zinnia Second Floor

The Zinnia Front Elevation

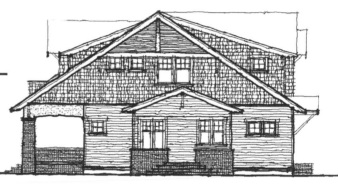

The Zinnia Right Elevation

The Zinnia Rear Elevation

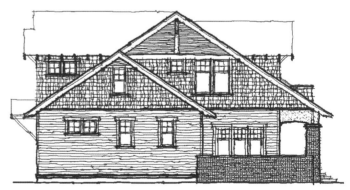

The Zinnia Left Elevation

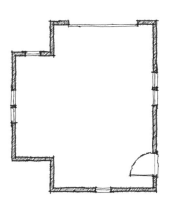

The Petunia Garage

The Petunia

Total: 378 square feet

The Petunia is designed to work as a coordinating garage for the Zinnia. The single-car garage is designed for a midsized wagon and bicycle parking. The garage may be located to load from the front of the street or to be reversed and load from an alley. Small multiple roof forms help keep the scale of the building from competing visually, while identical design details create a cohesive design vocabulary.

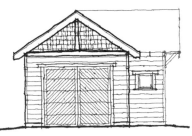

The Petunia Front Elevation

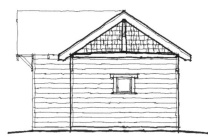

The Petunia Rear Elevation

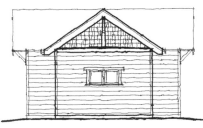

The Petunia Right Elevation

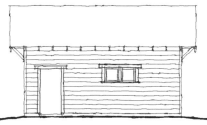

The Petunia Left Elevation

The Petunia

The Tulip

THE TULIP

FIRST FLOOR: 933 SQUARE FEET
SECOND FLOOR: 763 SQUARE FEET
TOTAL: 1,696 SQUARE FEET

This is a Prairie-style bungalow designed to work on a rural or urban lot. A small formal entry connects to the living room or a home office. Living room, dining room and kitchen connect through cased openings and provide a sense of separation while maintaining a visual connection throughout the home. The kitchen integrates a built-in eating nook, chef's desk and pantry. The laundry room is conveniently located adjacent to the kitchen and serves as a side entry/mudroom to the home. The second floor houses two bedrooms with a Jack and Jill bath and a master suite that connects to a second-floor deck.

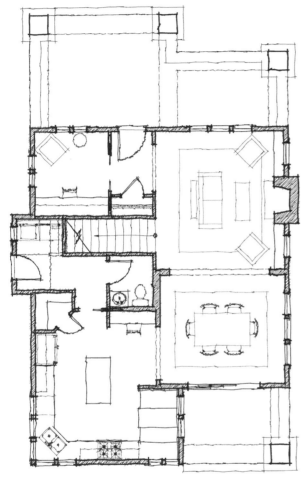

The Tulip First Floor

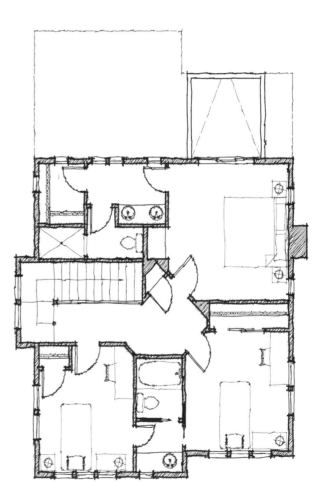

The Tulip Second Floor

The Tulip Front Elevation

The Tulip Right Elevation

The Tulip Rear Elevation

The Tulip Left Elevation

The Peony

First floor: 899 square feet
Second floor: 489 square feet
Total: 1,388 square feet

A small rural retreat or urban oasis, the Peony provides ample outdoor living space with a full front porch, side patio with pergola and a covered porch and patio off the kitchen. The entry provides a space to decompress from the elements and connects to the living room, which integrates a corner-mounted fireplace and french doors to the patio. The efficient kitchen integrates a built-in eating nook with seating for six, surrounded by windows maximizing light and view into the home. The main-floor master suite is located on the right-hand side of the house and connects to the rear patio, completing a courtyard-inspired plan for the backyard. Laundry and pantry spaces are located adjacent to the kitchen and master bedroom. The second floor includes a well-lit scissors stair that connects to a central hall with access to one bedroom, and a secondary flexible living space that can be used as a den or auxiliary sleeping space. Both second-floor rooms have private access to a shared bathroom.

The Peony

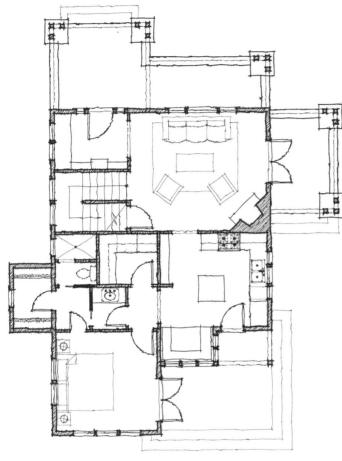

The Peony First Floor

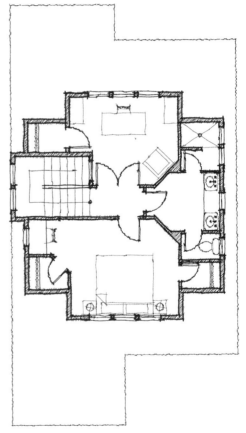

The Peony Second Floor

The Peony Front Elevation

The Peony Rear Elevation

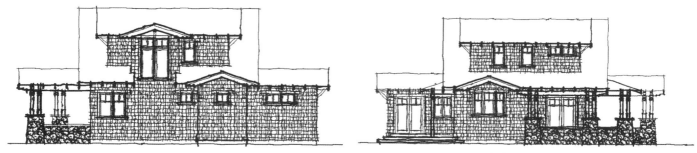

The Peony Right Elevation

The Peony Left Elevation

The Sweet Pea

THE SWEET PEA

GARAGE FLOOR:
504 SQUARE FEET
SECOND FLOOR:
381 SQUARE FEET
TOTAL: 885 SQUARE FEET

Designed to accompany the Peony house, this oversized single-car garlow provides generous parking space for one car with additional storage for kayaks, bikes or a small workshop. The second floor is accessed with an exterior stair and can be used as a small guest suite, apartment or at-home office.

The Sweet Pea Front Elevation

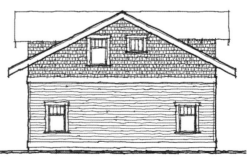
The Sweet Pea Right Elevation

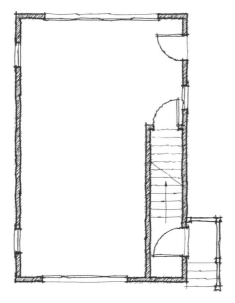

The Sweet Pea Garage Floor

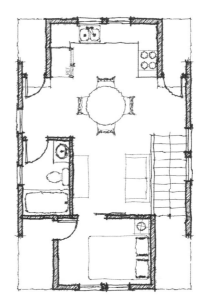

The Sweet Pea Second Floor

The Sweet Pea Rear Elevation

The Sweet Pea Left Elevation

The Fox Tail

First floor: 674 square feet
Second floor: 527 square feet
Total: 1,201 square feet

This traditionally inspired, shed-roof bungalow includes full front porch with tapered wood columns and relieved porch balusters. The entry, equipped with a built-in bench and coat hooks, leads to the living room with full masonry wood-burning fireplace. The well-appointed kitchen is open to the living room and is separated with a large cased opening. An eat-in kitchen nook provides circulation to a covered porch for access to the backyard.

The laundry center and powder room have direct access to the outdoors and circulate into the home through the compartmentalized at-home work area. The winding stair integrates light from upstairs to the living room and provides access to the two upstairs bedrooms. The master suite includes a full bath with walk-in shower and window seat. Access to a small roof deck from the master suite creates territorial views to the backyard. The secondary bedroom includes a small bath, built-in bookshelves and access to a large deck overlooking the front yard.

The Fox Tail

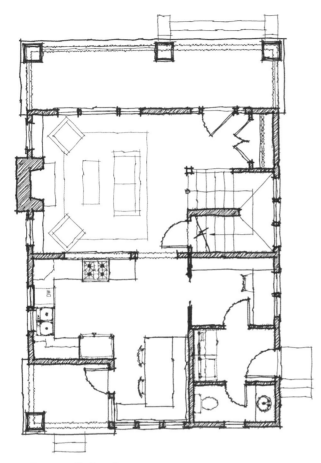

The Fox Tail First Floor

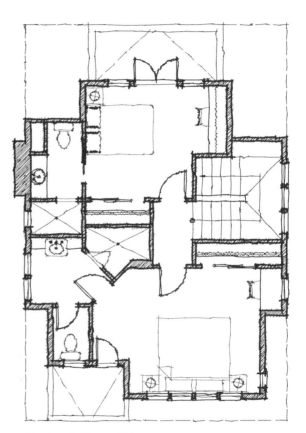

The Fox Tail Second Floor

The Fox Tail Front Elevation

The Fox Tail Right Elevation

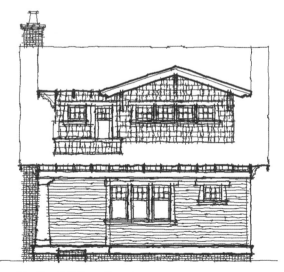

The Fox Tail Rear Elevation

The Fox Tail Left Elevation

SMALL BUNGALOW PLANS—ILLUSTRATED **91**

The Hyacinth

THE HYACINTH

FIRST FLOOR: 744 SQUARE FEET
SECOND FLOOR: 910 SQUARE FEET
TOTAL HOME: 1,654 SQUARE FEET
GARAGE: 231 SQUARE FEET

Designed to work on a traditional infill lot, the Hyacinth has a small covered front porch that leads into an entry with a coat closet and stairs to the second floor. The living space is abundant with natural light as the fireplace is located on an interior wall, maximizing the connection to the outdoors. The dining room is centered between the living room and kitchen and has covered access to the outdoors. The kitchen includes a walk-in pantry and ample cabinet space. The mudroom connects to a small single-car garage that is accessed off the side of the home.

The shotgun stair leads to the second floor that includes two modest bedrooms and a master suite. The master suite and secondary bedrooms are separated by a play area for children. The two bedrooms share a bathroom, which is located adjacent to the laundry area.

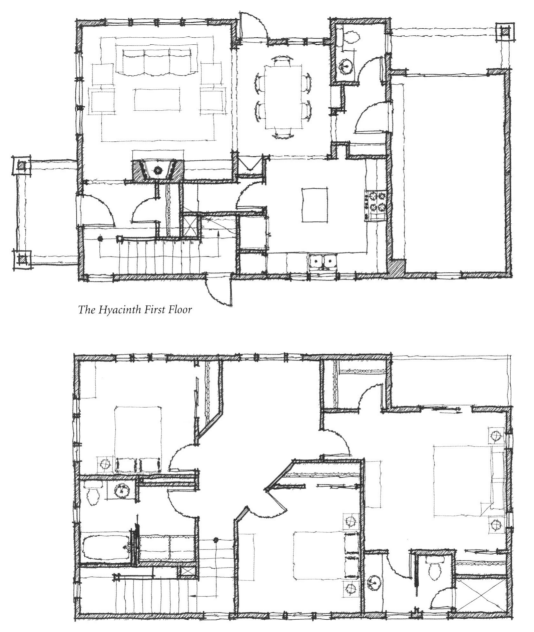

The Hyacinth First Floor

The Hyacinth Second Floor

The Hyacinth Front Elevation

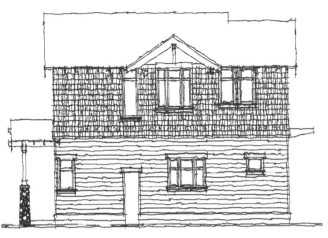

The Hyacinth Right Elevation

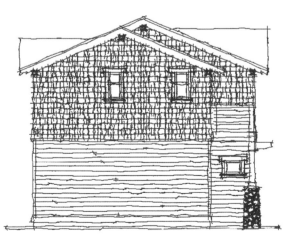

The Hyacinth Rear Elevation

The Hyacinth Left Elevation

The Lily

First floor: 810 square feet
Second floor: 582 square feet
Total: 1,392 square feet

The Lily bungalow is signified by its shed roof; with its two juxta-posed gable dormers, it creates an asymmetrical building form. The front covered porch provides direct access to the entry or an out-of-the-way space to enjoy the yard. The center stair located at the rear of the living room provides access to the second floor. The living room has a centered fireplace and is flanked by two windows with bookcases below. The U-shaped kitchen is directly adjacent to the living room and includes a two-person nook. The dining room is located to the rear of the kitchen, with access to an outdoor patio. The mudroom has a full bath and flows to a gracious den or small bedroom. The second-floor master suite includes a full bath and walk-in closet. The second bedroom has a full bath and large in-room closet. The hallway serves as a secondary at-home work space with a built-in desk and work area.

The Lily

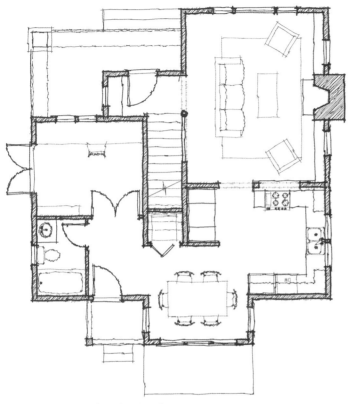

The Lily First Floor

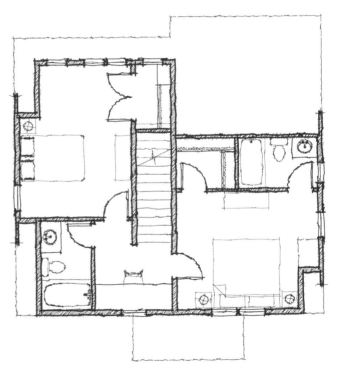

The Lily Second Floor

The Lily Front Elevation

The Lily Right Elevation

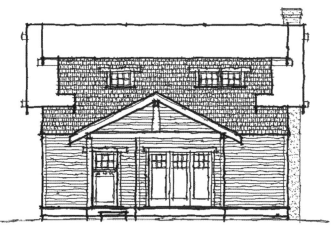

The Lily Rear Elevation

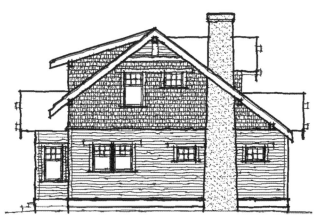

The Lily Left Elevation

The Sea Grass

THE SEA GRASS
First floor: 543 square feet
Second floor: 316 square feet
Total: 859 square feet

This small one-bedroom retreat includes an entry that flows into a great room; it incorporates the living room and kitchen into one open space. The dining area is a nook with windows on all sides, which maximizes light and the view to the exterior. A small mud-room doubles as a laundry center and at-home work space while providing access to a first-floor powder room. The winding stair connects to the second-floor master suite. The master suite provides a full bathroom with a walk-in shower and closet. The master bedroom includes a full window seat and exterior roof deck.

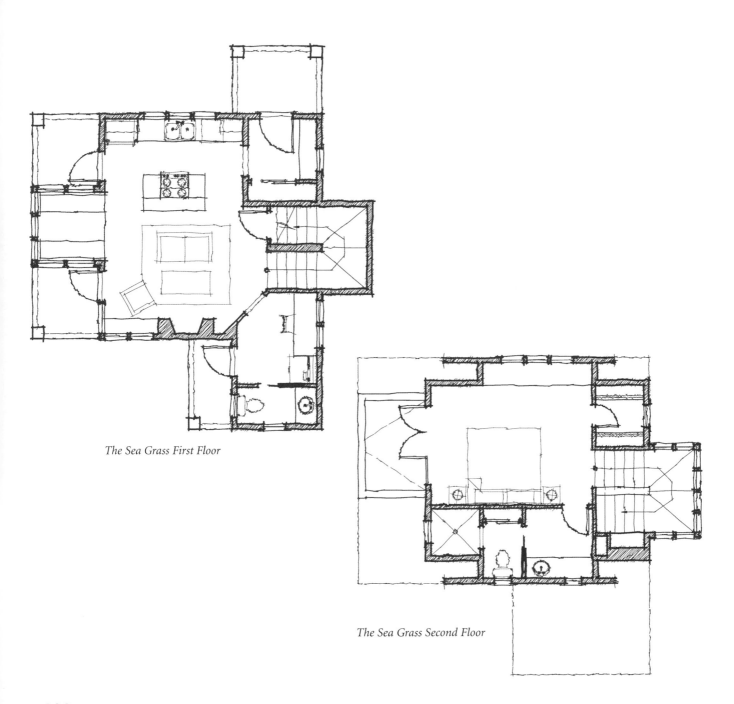

The Sea Grass First Floor

The Sea Grass Second Floor

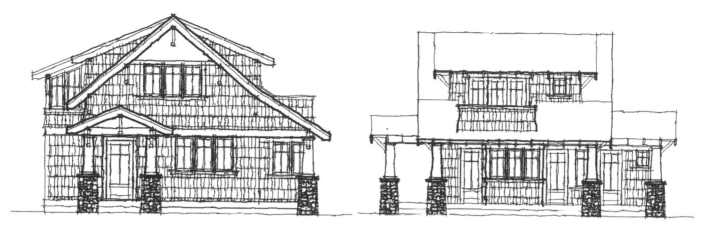

The Sea Grass Front Elevation

The Sea Grass Right Elevation

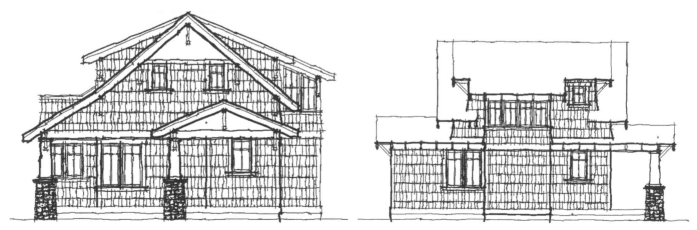

The Sea Grass Rear Elevation

The Sea Grass Left Elevation

The Larkspur

First floor: 1,094 square feet
Second floor: 537 square feet
Total: 1,631 square feet

Low-pitched roofs with large overhangs are reminiscent of Greene and Greene homes designed in southern California in the early 1900s. The rock-and-brick columns grow out of the earth, connecting the porch to the landscape. The entry provides a space to store coats and connects to the living room. The living room contains a centered fireplace, doors to the front porch and french doors to a den or dining room. The kitchen, adjacent to the living room, is well appointed and features a diagonal eating nook that focuses on the backyard. The laundry room and powder room are located next to the kitchen and create a vestibule that provides access to the main-floor master suite with walk-in closet. The second floor is comprised of two large bedrooms with a shared bathroom. The second bedroom has access to a second-floor roof deck that surveys the backyard.

The Larkspur

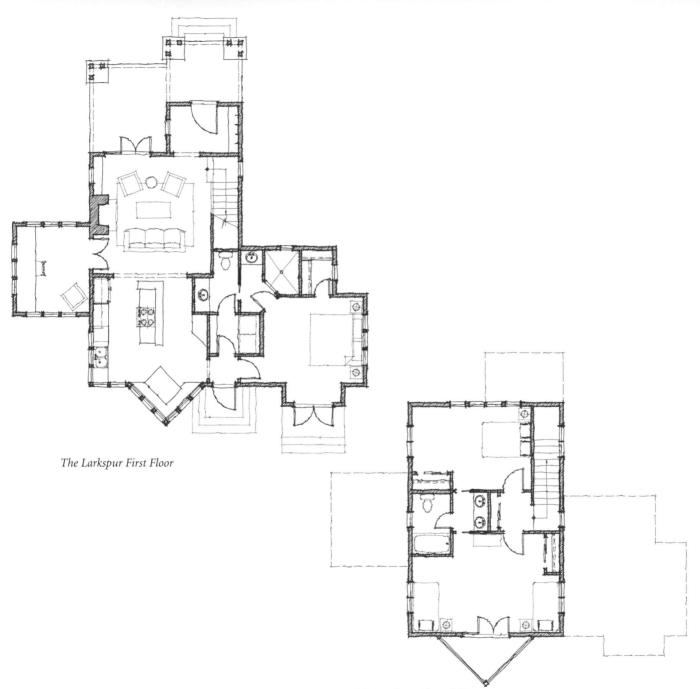

The Larkspur First Floor

The Larkspur Second Floor

The Larkspur Front Elevation

The Larkspur Right Elevation

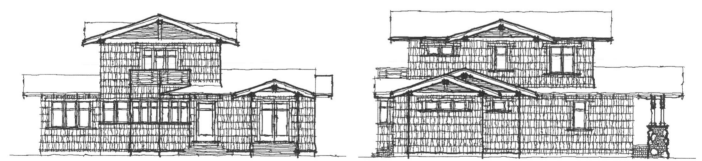

The Larkspur Rear Elevation

The Larkspur Left Elevation

These designs are part of a greater collection of those available at The Bungalow Company. Visit www.bungalowcompany.com, or call 888-945-9206 for plan and pricing details.

RESOURCES

Author

Christian Gladu
The Bungalow Company
PO Box 584
Bend, OR 97709
(888) 945-9206
www.bungalowcompany.com

Photography

Ross Chandler
Chandler Photography
739 NE 10th Street
Bend, OR 97701
(541) 385-3185
www.chandlerphoto.com

Architectural Illustration

Rob Leanna
41 Green Street
Newburyport, MA 01950
(978) 465-1095
robleanna@comcast.net

Accessories

Trimbelle River Studio & Design
PO Box 568
Ellsworth, WI 54011
(715) 273-4844
www.trimbelleriver.com

Associations

(APA) The Engineered Wood Association
7011 S. 19th Street
Tacoma, WA 98466
(253) 565-6600
www.apawood.org

Cedar Shake & Shingle Bureau
PO Box 1178
Sumas, WA 98295
(604) 820-7700
www.cedarbureau.org

Energy & Environmental Building Association
10740 Lyndale Avenue South,
Suite 10W
Bloomington, MN 55420
(952) 881-1098
www.eeba.org

Environmental Building News— Building Green, Inc.
122 Birge Street, Suite 30
Brattleboro, VT 05301
(802) 257-7300
www.buildinggreen.com

National Association of Home Builders
1201–15th Street NW
Washington, D.C. 20005
(800) 368-5242
www.nahb.com

Western Red Cedar Lumber Association
1501–700 W. Pender Street
Pender Place 1, Business Building
Vancouver, BC, Canada V6C 1G8
(866) 778-909
www.wrcla.org

(WWPA) Western Wood Products Association
522 SW Fifth Avenue, Suite 500
Portland, OR 97204
(503) 224-3930
www.wwpa.org

Window & Door Manufacturers Association
1400 E. Touhy Avenue, Suite 470
Des Plaines, IL 60018
(800) 223-2301
www.wdma.com

Builders

Arts & Crafts Builders
3 Bethesda Metro Center, Suite 700
Bethesda, MD 20814
(301) 325-4914
www.artsandcraftsbuilders.com

Bethesda Bungalows
5126 Fairglen Lane
Chevy Chase, MD 20815
(240) 464-3137
www.bethesdabungalows.com

Greg Welch Construction
816 NW Fort Clatsop Street
Bend, OR 97701
(541) 420-1497

Ironwood Construction
PO Box 571
Bend, OR 97709
(541) 318-1025

Mike Knighten Construction
3567 McCready Drive
Bend, OR 97701
(541) 317-9636
www.mikeknighten-construction.com

Sunco Development
PO Box 7944
Bend, OR 97709
(541) 383-1926

Tom Tanner Construction
715 NW Yosemite Drive
Bend, OR 97701
(541) 410-3220

Bungalow Plans

The Bungalow Company
PO Box 584
Bend, OR 97709
(888) 945-9206
www.bungalowcompany.com

Cabinets

Crown Point Cabinetry
PO BOX 1560
Claremont, NH 03743
(800) 999-4994
www.crown-point.com

Harvest Moon Woodworks
Bend, OR
(541) 330-3960

FIREPLACES

Buckley Rumford Company
1035 Monroe Street
Port Townsend, WA 98368
(360) 385-9974
www.rumford.com

Chimney Pot Shoppe
1915 Brush Run Road
Avella, PA 15312
(724) 345-3601
www.chimneypot.com

Moberg Fireplaces, Inc.
Cellar Building, Suite 300
1124 NW Couch Street
Portland, OR 97209
(503) 227-0547
www.mobergfireplaces.com

Town & Country Fireplaces
(888) 223-0088
www.townandcountryfireplaces.net

FLOORING

**Armstrong World Industries—
DLW Linoleum**
PO Box 3001
Lancaster, PA 17604
(800) 233-3823
www.armstrong.com

**Emerson Hardwood Floors/Cross
Cut Hardwoods**
3738 NW Yeon
Portland, OR 97210
(800) 820 9898
www.emersonhardwood.com

Teragren
12715 Miller Road NE, Suite 301
Bainbridge Island, WA 98110
(800) 929-6333
www.teragren.com

GARAGE DOORS

Designer Doors
702 Troy Street
River Falls, WI 54022
(800) 241-0525
www.designerdoors.com

HARDWARE

**The Bungalow Gutter
Bracket Co.**
PO Box 22144
Lexington, KY 40522
(859) 335-1555
www.bungalowgutterbracket.com

Chown Hardware
333 NW 16th Avenue
Portland, OR 97209
(800) 547-1930
www.chown.com

Craftsman Hardware
PO Box 351
Arlington, WA 98223
(425) 483-2826
www.craftsmanhardware.com

**Craftsmen Hardware Company,
Ltd.**
PO Box 161
Marceline, MO 64658
(660) 376-2481
www.craftsmenhardware.com

Crown City Hardware
1047 N. Allen Avenue
Pasadena, CA 91104
(626) 794-0234
www.crowncityhardware.com

EmTek Decorative Hardware
(800) 356-2741
www.emtekproducts.com

**Rockler Woodworking &
Hardware**
(800) 279 4441
www.rockler.com

INSERTS & STOVES

Heat & Glow
20802 Kensington Boulevard
Lakeville, MN 55044
(888) 427-3973
www.heatnglo.com

Vermont Castings
410 Admiral Boulevard
Mississauga, ON, Canada
L5T 2N6
(800) 525-1898
www.vermontcastings.com

WINDOWS & DOORS

Andersen Windows & Doors
Andersen Corporation
100 Fourth Avenue North
Bayport, MN 55003
(800) 426-4261
www.andersenwindows.com

Buffelen Woodworking Company
PO Box 1383
Tacoma, WA 98401
(253) 627-1191
www.buffelendoor.com

International Door & Latch
1455 Westec Drive
Eugene, OR 97402
(541) 686-5647
www.internationaldoor.com

Jeld-WEN Windows & Doors
(800) 535-3936
www.jeld-wen.com

Marvin Windows & Doors
PO Box 100
Warroad, MN 56763
(888) 537-7828
www.marvin.com

Sierra Pacific Windows
(800) 824-7744
www.sierrapacificwindows.com

Simpson Door Company
400 Simpson Avenue
McCleary, WA 98557
(800) 952-4057
www.simpsondoor.com

INTERIOR FINISH MATERIAL
Environmental Building Supplies
819 SE Taylor Street
Portland, OR 97214
(503) 222-3881
www.ecohaus.com

Environmental Home Center
4121–1st Avenue South
Seattle, WA 98134
(800) 281-9785
www.built-e.com

McCoy Millwork
342 SE Caruthers Street
Portland, OR 97214
(888) 236-0995
www.mccoymillwork.com

Shelter Supply, Inc.
151 East Cliff Road, Suite 30
Burnsville, MN 55337
(800) 762-8399
www.sheltersupply.com

INTERIOR FURNISHINGS
The Craftsman Home
3048 Claremont Avenue
Berkeley, CA 94705
(510) 655-6503
www.craftsmanhome.com

The Craftsman Homes Connection
2525 E. 29th Street, Suite 10B-343
Spokane, WA 99223
(509) 535-5098
www.crafthome.com

L. & J. G. Stickley, Inc.
1 Stickley Drive
PO Box 480
Manlius, NY 13104
(315) 682-5500
www.stickley.com

Michael Fitzsimmons Decorative Arts
311 W. Superior Street
Chicago, IL 60610
(312) 787-0496
www.fitzdecarts.com

Modern Bungalow
2594 S. Colorado Boulevard
at Yale U Hills Plaza
Denver, CO 80222
(303) 300-3332
www.modernbungalow.com

LIGHTING
Craftsmen Lighting by Craftsmen Hardware Company, Ltd.
PO Box 161
Marceline, MO 64658
(660) 376-2481
www.craftsmenhardware.com

Historic Lighting
114 E. Lemon Avenue
Monrovia, CA 91016
(888) 757-9770
www.historiclighting.com

Old California Lantern Company
975 N. Enterprise Street
Orange, CA 92867
(800) 577-6679
www.oldcalifornia.com

Rejuvenation Lamp & Fixture Company
2550 NW Nicolai Street
Portland, OR 97210
(888) 401-1900
www.rejuvenation.com

School House Electric
330 SE MLK Jr. Boulevard
Portland, OR 97214
(800) 630-7113
www.schoolhouseelectric.com

PAINT
Benjamin Moore
www.benjaminmoore.com

Historic House Colors
Robert Schweitzer
3661 Waldenwood Drive
Ann Arbor, MI 48105
(734) 668-0298
www.historichousecolors.com

Sherwin-Williams
www.sherwin-williams.com

PERIODICALS

American Bungalow
PO Box 756
123 S. Baldwin Avenue
Sierra Madre, CA 91024
(800) 350-3363
www.ambungalow.com

Arts & Crafts Homes and the Revival
Gloucester Publishers
108 E. Main Street
Gloucester, MA 01930
(978) 283-3200
www.artsandcraftshomes.com

Builder
One Thomas Circle NW, Suite 600
Washington, D.C. 20005
(202) 452-0800
www.builderonline.com

Fine Homebuilding
The Taunton Press
63 S. Main Street
PO Box 5506
Newtown, CT 06470
(800) 477-8727
www.finehomebuilding.com

New Old House
Restore Media, LLC
1000 Potomac Street NW,
Suite 102
Washington, D.C. 20007
(202) 339-0744
www.restoremedia.com

The Journal of Light Construction
186 Allen Brook Lane
Williston, VT 05495
(802) 879-3335
www.jlconline.com

PLUMBING

A-ball Plumbing Supply
1703 W. Burnside Street
Portland, OR 97209
(800) 228-0134
www.a-ball.com

Kohler
444 Highland Drive
Kohler, WI 53044
(800) 456-4537
www.kohler.com

ROOF

ELK Building Products
www.elkcorp.com

Owens Corning
www.owenscorning.com

SIDING & TRIM

Bear Creek Lumber
PO Box 669
Winthrop, WA 98862
(800) 597-7191
www.bearcreeklumber.com

James Hardie
26300 La Alameda Drive,
Suite 250
Mission Viejo, CA 92691
(888) 542-7343
www.jameshardie.com

Lakeside Lumber
10600 SW Tualatin
Sherwood Road
Tualatin, OR 97062
(877) 877-8319
www.lakesidelumber.com

TILE

Motawi Tile Works
170 Enterprise Drive
Ann Arbor, MI 48103
(734) 213-0017
www.motawi.com

Norberry Tile
Seattle Design Center, Suite 221
5701–6th Avenue South
Seattle, WA 98108
(206) 343-9916
www.norberrytile.com

Pratt & Larson Ceramics
1201 SE 3rd Avenue
Portland, OR 97214
(503) 231-9464
www.prattandlarson.com

Tile Restoration Center
3511 Interlake Avenue North
Seattle, WA 98103
(206) 633-4866
www.tilerestorationcenter.com